TEN THINGS I WISH I'D KNOWN ABOUT NETWORK MARKETING BEFORE I GOT STARTED

(By someone who made it)

Cristina Williams

TEN THINGS I WISH I'D KNOWN ABOUT NETWORK MARKETING BEFORE I GOT STARTED
(by someone who made it)

Copyright © 2022 Cristina Williams
First published 2022

Disruptive Publishing
17 Spencer Avenue
Deception Bay QLD 4508
Australia
WEB: www.disruptivepublishing.com.au

Editing Services by Jandyco
Book Cover by Disruptive Publishing
Layout by Jandyco
Cover Image by Chad Weed @ Chad J Weed Photography

ISBN# 978-0-6455278-5-8 Print

To my amazing husband, Mat. Who I love a ridiculous amount.

To our seven beautiful boys. Who make our life an obscene amount of fun.

And to you, the reader. Thank you for sitting with me and allowing me to share a little part of your journey.

Foreword

Some people are solo travelers through life. Not Cristina. She's determined to take others along, ensuring they savor every new experience and squeeze the juice out of every adventure.

I've hacked my way through the Amazon rainforest both with, and without, a guide to follow. Trust me, it's easier and more enjoyable when an experienced guide can show you the way ... pointing out the wonders you may otherwise miss, warning of unseen dangers, preventing missteps, saving time, and conserving your valuable energy.

To the uninitiated, network marketing can be a jungle. It's not easy, nor should it be. It's an entrepreneurial trek most worthy of your time, energy, and diligent effort. Its rewards are rich in life experience, relationships forged, and the best of true success, no matter how you define it.

Cristina is not only a brilliant student of life; she's an extraordinary teacher. Learn from her! Her wisdom and life example will shorten your learning curve, will clear the underbrush from your path, will help you overcome the inevitable obstacles you'll face and lead you to the sweet summit of success that no other endeavor can offer like the noble, fair, and most rewarding profession of network marketing.

Ed Wiens

Global Entrepreneur
40 Year Networking Veteran
Multi-Million Dollar Earner

Table of Contents

Introduction

I know this book has a long title. I'm sorry about that. But I really wanted you to know exactly what the book is about and why it could really make a difference to anyone hoping to get real results in this industry.

But don't stress—this is not going to be a long book. I already know you don't have the time to read it, and I probably don't have the time to write it. So, it's more of an instruction manual, helping you to drive this new crazy gig you just jumped into ... or are thinking of getting into. But the things in here *need* to be said, because they TRULY would have made a difference to me getting results faster and I KNOW they can make a big difference to you too as you get started.

Why do I want to write this book? Actually, because I care about you. Because I've met you before. After 20 years in network marketing, I've seen so many excited hopefuls get started—bringing their deepest dreams to the altar of the network marketing gods, hoping that this truly might work. Many will have great success, many will not. The key, however, is that anyone CAN.

I wish I had a magic wand that would guarantee success to wave over everyone getting started. Since I don't, however, I would like to give you Ten Tips that will stack the odds massively in your favor ... so that your new business really might give you everything you're hoping for and more.

We don't know what we don't know—and that's dangerous!

How different life might have been if someone had shared these truths with me all those years ago, when I first made my timid debut onto the network marketing scene. I might have been successful sooner; I might have been less scared. I might have been able to enjoy the process and get better results. I would have suffered less, for sure.

It might have saved me ten years!

So, let's do this. Let me share with you the ten things I wish I'd known about network marketing before I got started … now that I can finally say I've climbed successfully to the six-figure summit—*twice.*

My first leap into network marketing was in my twenties. I'm not going to name companies in this book, because principles are principles. They apply no matter what product, service, or concept you are promoting. The company was well established, I was a young new bride with big hopes for my life ahead. My first husband and I built to the top ranks of that company and lived an amazing life for ten years, travelling the world and making many dreams come true.

It was a rockstar lifestyle, no doubt about it. I've met many people in my life who are wealthy and have had great success in different fields. But I've *never* seen anyone live the kind of life a successful network marketer does. *None.* The time, the money, the freedom, the balance, and choices—forget it, there is nothing else like it. That's just a fact.

But sadly, our marriage fell apart, and so did the business. It would be a waste of time and energy to go back and try to figure out whose fault was what—the fact is we both could have done things better, and certainly the company we were with could have done things better. But at the end of the day, we all have to take responsibility for the decisions we make. It was *my* life; *I* had made those choices—and they hadn't worked out.

And so, I found myself at the age of 30: alone, raising four young boys under five, no money, no education, no prospects, no safety net and to be honest, I was a total mess. I had tumbled down from a life of luxury, to scavenging through the Goodwill bins at our local church for clothes my children could wear.

I had taken nothing with me but the clothes on my back when I walked out of my million-dollar lifestyle. My boys and I slept on mattresses on the floor for a few months, inside our little shoe box rental on a main road. My ex had lost everything too and so it wasn't for lack of wanting, but he too had no way to help. We were both lost. I would watch my babies sleep at night and quietly vowed that I would find a way to pull our life back together. Although I had no idea how.

It's funny how many friends I seemed to have when I had money. How many people were happy to come to the parties we'd throw at the gorgeous house we'd lavishly decorated. There was never a shortage of people wanting to drink our expensive wine, come travelling and laugh into the night. And now, there was silence. Not a single sound. No phone calls or knocks at the door to see if my boys and I were alright.

I was alone. It was sobering and it was cruel.

Yet in retrospect, that season of struggle was an important rebirth that I desperately needed in an emotional and spiritual sense. That trying time would eventually lead me towards the *best* part of my life, because in those quiet nights of desperation is where my resolve was born. The promises I made to my little boys turned out to be the fiery oath from where I drew the strength to fight back. Inside those flames, is where I finally grew up.

The 'time in the desert' was not short and it was not easy. For almost eight years I struggled to find a way to make a comeback. I juggled many jobs, I reinvented myself more times than I can count. One minute I was a waitress, the next I was the managing director of a marketing firm. Then a minute later, a waitress again.

I had little ideas, big ideas and most of the time—*no idea*. But all along, something was niggling at me—and it was the fact that I'd already had a taste of the kind of life that network marketing could provide. And no matter what else I tried, I hadn't found *anything* that could come even remotely close.

Sure, it takes work to build a network marketing business … but I was working twice as hard already in every other kind of business I tried. With network marketing I knew at least that if I built it properly, a business like that could continue to yield for years ... and, nurtured well, forever.

But I had so many doubts. Did I have the energy to climb the mountain again? Could I do it alone this time? Did I still have magic in me ... *did I ever have it?* Were my best days behind me? Had I already missed my chance?

And just as I was beginning to open up again to the possibility of coming back into the industry, an opportunity with an amazing company came my way, and it was perfect. So, I did the only thing sensible people do—I tried to talk myself out of it. I thought of every excuse why it wouldn't work and why, specifically, it wouldn't work for *me*.

I turned it around and around in my head for almost a year (I know, shocker!) until finally one day I had no choice. Not because I was inspired or because I was ready. Nobody is ever really ready. I got started because I was desperate.

The small business I had built was going backwards in a hurry, I was running out of money fast, my children were growing up even faster and I had had ENOUGH. Just like that, I was done. Done struggling, done crying, done having a hard life.

I didn't care what I had to do anymore, I just knew I HAD to do SOMETHING to change our lives.

***

I don't know who you are, but I already know one very important thing about you by the fact that you have this book in your hands.

You want to change your life too.

I'm not saying you 'hate' your life. Even through my toughest times, I've never hated my life. I've always found something to be grateful for. BUT we all come to a crossroad; a moment in time which is like an inflection point. Even if you don't quite realise it at the time, you will look back on it in years to come and say, "THAT was the moment I made THE decision".

It shouldn't take your whole life, to change your whole life.

Tony Robbins, the great motivational master, says that profound change can happen in one moment ... though sometimes it can take us years to work up to that moment! So maybe that's why you're here: because that moment for you is right now.

And although your life will not entirely change in an instant, you know with every cell in your body, that it *will*. Your circumstances have begun to shift because your mind has taken the first step. You've made eye contact with your future self and it's just a matter of time until your reality catches up.

We don't get in life what we want. We get in life exactly what we expect.

You're done waiting, you're done watching. You're ready to make this happen. In fact, it's already done ... even if you're not quite sure how.

That's where I can help.

It doesn't matter what company you've chosen to work with—there are principles that are consistent across our industry and across every success story that has walked the network marketing stage. Walking into my second company with these principles in hand, I was able to build a six-figure income and reach the major rank in my company within just one year. And I have continued to grow to heights that have far surpassed the success of my twenties.

And yet, I am nothing special. I was just a single mom with a dream. A heart filled with hope and the desire to fight for my boys. You can have it all too: the income, the time freedom, the success, the recognition, and personal satisfaction a winner feels when he or she achieves what they set out to do.

In one year, I promise you that you can transform your life.

It doesn't need to take more. One year is enough to turn the ship around and get yourself headed in a whole new direction to a life of abundance and clarity. To a life where your dreams are not images stuck to your fridge, but experiences you hold in your hands.

I encourage you to open your heart to these ten truths to follow. They will each serve you in instrumental ways to help you reach your mountaintop faster, with less pain and with more joy.

See you at the top.

Cristina

CHAPTER ONE

It works!

Getting started in any business can be challenging. It doesn't matter if you're opening a restaurant, or a store, or launching a network marketing career—the fact is that there is one great question that is probably nagging you the most: *will this work?*

When I started building my network marketing business several years ago, I was a single mom with four young boys, a busy job, and a seemingly endless list of problems to solve. I did not need another headache. I could not afford to waste my time. I really needed to know if there was a real chance that the opportunity I was exploring could work.

*What I was really, **really** asking, was: "Could this work for **me**?"*

In case you're asking yourself the same question, let me give you some cold hard facts. The network marketing industry turns over in excess of US$189 billion (yes, that's BILLION with a B!!) in sales every year. There are currently 166 million people actively engaged in the industry in over 100 countries around the world.

Of these distributors, the average income for a high-ranking associate (Diamond or equivalent) is US$99,975 per year—while the median income in the United States of

America is US$31,133 (2022). Approximately $800 billion has been paid out in commissions over the last ten years and a successful network marketer comfortably out-earns any of the top three professions in the United States of America (US) today (2022): Anesthesiologists (US$261,730), General Surgeons (US$252,040) and Maxillofacial Surgeons (US$237,570).

For comparison, the median income in my current company, for my current rank is US$493,068 per year.

Those numbers say a LOT.

Yes, networking marketing can be a little part-time hustle, but it can also be a big-time profession with a *big-time income*. The critical difference is that in network marketing what you earn is up to YOU. Regardless of how hard you work in any other profession, from a waitress to a maxillofacial surgeon, what you earn is generally up to someone else. Don't you just hate that?

My husband, Mat, has been a classic example. He works in Senior Management in the corporate sector, and even though he worked his guts out for more than a decade for one particular corporation, there was absolutely no way for him to advance or lift his income further. His boss, meanwhile, worked very similar hours and yet got paid, literally ten times what my husband made. He has recently changed jobs, but essentially ANY company he works for will always feature the same scenario: the people 'above' him will make more money, regardless of who puts in more effort. That's what an *actual* pyramid looks like, friends.

Wait a minute—not everyone is making money in network marketing, you say. And that is true. Hold on, stop! Did someone tell you that *everybody* who gets into network marketing is successful?? I'm sorry if you got that impression—let me clear it right up: not everyone who gets into network marketing is wildly successful. You know why? Because network marketing is part of the real world; and in the real world, there is NOTHING in which EVERYONE is successful.

The truth is that there are people who don't make it in *every* industry. There are sad stories of small businesses that went bust, people who have lost millions in the share market, restaurants that folded after decades of hard work … there are no guarantees in any segment of the economy.

The biggest scam of all, in my opinion, is the lie we are fed through the education system: that if you want security, you need to get a job. I've never quite connected the dots on that one. How is working for 40 years and ending up in retirement trying to live off less than US$24,000 per year (USA median retirement income 2021) a success story?

No. Not everyone makes it in network marketing, just like not everyone makes it in every other industry either *[insert violin music here]*. If you're looking for a business with a guarantee, you're looking for a unicorn, my friend.

Now that we've got that out of the way, let's remember that if others failed at something it's actually of little relevance to you. Some people make it, some people don't … who cares?

What you really want to know when evaluating a business is not how you compare to other people, but how the business compares to your other *options*.

So, let's replace the question, *'Will I be successful in network marketing?'* with a better question: *'What are my chances of being successful **without** network marketing?'*

Have you noticed that the naysayers always avoid evaluating your other options? They'll happily trash network marketing, but they won't offer you a different solution to get out of your financial nightmare. I heard it said once, "Don't ever take advice or counsel from someone who hasn't already got the life you want, and who isn't willing to help you get it".

When the comparison is made, there isn't a job in the world, not even a fancy maxillofacial surgeon, that can offer you the full lifestyle rewards of network marketing. But I digress ... network marketing is not a *job*; it is a **business** (more on this later). Any business takes time to establish. If you're coming in red-hot hoping to retire on your first paycheck, this is not the gig for you. Hopefully you already know that!

What you probably want to know is: *'If I put the effort in, will it be worth it?'*

The tough reality is that it's a zoo out there. Even inside your own company, there are probably people doing really well and others with absolutely no idea what they're in! And then there's your brother-in-law Frank, who was probably in something similar back in college, and he's got stories that will make you weep.

Then of course, there's the keyboard warriors. People sitting at home behind the anonymity of their computer screens, tearing down anyone who is having a go. They don't know you, they don't know a thing about your life— but they're happy to tell you that you're wrong. Who *are* these people? Who has the time to be so negative and cruel?

I don't know who they are, but I'll tell you who they are *not*. They are not wildly successful. They are not daring entrepreneurs. They are not leaders or change makers. They are stuck in their lives, and they'll do anything to try to justify it, including pulling you down too.

Be careful who you listen to. When I was getting started, I wasn't interested in the stories of people who tanked out, or people who had a theory about why I'd never make it … I wanted to know the facts about the people who made it. What did they do? How long did it take? What were they earning?

What did they do, and what did they get?

As simple as that. I've always been prepared to put in the effort. I just needed tangible proof that it was possible and that the business model worked for those who worked it.

For those who really committed to being professionals in this industry, was it **worth it?**

Let's talk about what's really on offer. Some companies fare better than others, of course, but on average it takes an associate ten years to become a top income earner on a solid six-figure income. For the sake of comparison, let's talk about the other skin-slicing six-figure earners in the economy we mentioned earlier.

To become a surgeon in the US today you're looking at four to seven years of medical school, then three to seven years of residency and fellowships (depending on the specialty). Which means that to earn 'surgeon income' you'll have to put in at least 12 years of schooling ... and let's not forget that you'll also be taking home with you a lovely debt of anywhere between US$250,000 to US$500,000.

It's pretty much the same in any of the top professions: lawyers, CEOs, hedge fund managers, psychiatrists, mining engineers, orthodontists ... to name a few that score the big bucks. They also scored lots of years in study and big debts.

So, it bugs me that people say they've 'lost' money in network marketing ... but they don't blink when considering a cool US$200,000 for their education, which may or may not be helpful. The only way to 'lose' money in network marketing, is to quit before you've made it— which, incidentally, is what most people do.

If you're still with your company at the end of ten years, the stats tell us that you're most likely earning over six-figures. Sadly, the latest research shows that approximately 50% of network marketers quit within their first year, and over 95% will quit before ten years.

Guess what? If you quit medical school you're also not going to make any money! It's hard to cash in on something you abandoned. Life sucks like that. I quit the gym and my belly went back to being floppy. Dang! Yes, I'm devastated about not having rock-hard abs, but I don't sit around at every dinner party crying to my friends that, "I tried that thing", and to "look out for gyms, they're a scam. I can't believe they took my money, and I don't look like The Rock!".

We don't carry on like that because in most areas of our lives, we accept responsibility for our outcomes. Network marketing, however, is the magical place where people often feel excused from having to do that. It's the magical place where we feel entitled to claim that our lack of success was *definitely* everyone else's fault.

Curiously, when it comes to network marketing (and almost everything else) the recipe for success is surprisingly simple: stick with it! Stick with med school, stick with the sit ups. Stick with your business because those who stick it out are the ones who make *it*. Not just money, but in network marketing, they get the *lifestyle*. And that's the real prize because, blow me down, I'd take the lifestyle of a network marketer over that of a surgeon any day of the week.

Right now, as I write this chapter, I'm sitting on the balcony of an apartment my husband and I have rented for two weeks in a sleepy little seaside town near Barcelona, Spain. We got up this morning and hiked, we had a long lazy lunch overlooking the water, we dozed and read for hours on the sand. And yes, I'll also check in with my team and do a couple of meetings today ... before we take another stroll into the village for dinner.

Did I work to set up this lifestyle? Heck yes! Do I have to keep on working forever? Only if, and when, I choose to.

This is my fifth year with my current company. I'd only be halfway through med school and unlikely to ever replicate this lifestyle if I was chasing to create a comparable income through a job.

Okay, so we can safely establish that networking marketing is a more rewarding proposition than many of the top jobs in today's economy. But how does it compare to having your own business, you ask?

Buckle up!

A traditional small business is a real gamble when you explore the facts—something I already knew too well from personal experience. According to data from the US Bureau of Labor Statistics, about 20% of American small businesses fail within the first year. By the end of their fifth year, roughly 50% have faltered. After ten years, only around a third of businesses have survived. Hey, that doesn't sound too bad ... err, until you realise that the average small business owner still standing after ten years takes home approximately US$44,000 per year in personal revenue.

Gulp.

That's a lot of years, thousands of dollars invested, and a whole lot of risk to essentially end up earning about the same as any entry level job.

In essence, if I manage to tough it out for ten years in my small business (working long hours and investing tens of thousands of dollars each year) I could be rewarded by earning about the same as a fresh college graduate. Meanwhile, if I persevere and reach the ten-year mark in my network marketing business (that I paid a few hundred bucks to launch), I am statistically likely to be earning the same as the highest paid professions in the economy. BUT only work the hours I want?

Call me crazy, but did I really hesitate about this decision?

I was a struggling single mom. I didn't have the time or the brains to become a surgeon, I needed grocery money next week. I didn't have the years to launch my own small business, I didn't have thousands to invest into it, and I was uncertain if I'd even survive in it.

With the above in mind, let's go back and re-visit the question at the top of this chapter, "Does network marketing work?", and replace it with the real question.

"Does network marketing work **better** than my other options? Can it take me closer to my dreams, compared to my current job/business/investments?"

I concluded that there was nothing else that could give me the rewards of this industry. Those who launch themselves with that certainty are the ones who are willing to put in the work. And it's those who put in the work, and put in the time, who are the ones who, without fail, succeed.

Whatever prejudice, opinions, fears, or hesitations I might have had, when I stopped being a princess and looked at this objectively, the facts told me that this kind of business model was my best (and probably only) chance to turn around the financial mess I was in.

Understanding this from the start will save you a lot of time being scared and give you a lot more time being excited!

In the end, let's be real … it wasn't the industry I was doubting, it wasn't even the company or the product. What I was really concerned about was whether *I* could make it.

Little old me.

Fortunately, it's not about me. Just like it's not about *you*. The reality revealed by the numbers in this chapter is that ANYONE can make it. Anyone who decides to do the work, and to go the distance. Anyone who is ready for change. Anyone who thinks their family is worth it. Anyone who wants to live with choices, with freedom. Anyone who wants to make an impact and leave a positive footprint on the world.

Anyone who stops dipping their toes timidly in and out, and JUMPS IN.

Anyone with a dream.

Now, it's important to know that just because you know this, it doesn't mean that your friends and family automatically do. So, it's alright for them to be protective, it's alright that they might not understand.

And it's even alright if they don't want to follow.

I'm okay with the fact that many of my close friends do not want to do what I do. The truth is, I would not want to do what most of them do either. The idea of holding a nine to five job for the next 40 years is entirely unappealing to me. I am certain I couldn't be paid enough to subscribe to that plan. I respect them, I love them. But we're on different paths, and that's okay!

Live and let live. How can I be upset about someone not wanting to follow me, if I wouldn't want to follow them either?

Despite the opinions of the minority who still doubt that this robust, explosively expanding, multi-BILLION-dollar industry is real, you already know the truth: IT WORKS.

So, step into your business with that knowledge firmly secured under your belt. This is not an experiment; you aren't the first man or woman on the moon. You're stepping into a **proven business system** that continues to pump out the largest number of millionaires yearly, than almost any other industry.

So, stop acting like it's on trial. Don't you dare catch yourself wondering if 'it will work'. It already HAS for hundreds of thousands of people around the world, and it's growing bigger every single year.

The only question you have to ask isn't, *'Will the business work?'*

It's *'But will YOU?'*.

CHAPTER TWO

It's a business, not a job

It's very hard to cook a cake whilst following the recipe for pizza.

Sounds like a crazy statement. Well of course it is, but it is true.

Likewise, business building has principles. Business building has a particular mindset. If you come in with the right mindset and expectations, you will sail through. I'm not saying it will be easy, but you will find yourself working confidently and in flow.

On the other hand, the person who comes into network marketing with 'E Quadrant' thinking (employee mentality) will find themselves frequently frustrated and wrestling with results.

Even though you probably work with an incredible company and are most likely surrounded by an incredible field leadership team—be not confused, this is YOUR business. It's not your upline's business, or your company's business.

It truly is YOUR business and having this mindset makes all the difference to three key areas of how you perform:

1. Attitude

A business owner takes responsibility for his or her business. This sense of ownership is what drives you to take initiative and to lead, instead of waiting to be given instructions by someone superior.

You look to your upline team like coaches, not bosses. You're not out to impress anyone, but you're committed to impressing yourself. You wake up every morning searching for opportunities to grow and to nurture your business. You don't need anyone to tell you what to do. You're ASKING questions daily about your next steps.

You don't do things out of duty. You sow into your business out of pure joy. You don't stress about 'having' to do one more meeting. You're thrilled that you *get* to do one more and get a little closer every day to your dreams.

I remember working with a new person over several months; I felt a lot of compassion for her because, just like me, she was a single mom trying to find a way through for herself and her children. It seemed to me, however, that despite having a BIG reason to build a business, she was constantly negotiating with success. She was either too busy, or too tired, or too scared ... and one day she showed up to a meeting and told me that she had decided to quit. What she said next, however, was the really sad thing: "I'm sorry I've let you down".

Me? "Why have you let *me* down?", I asked her. It was *her* business, *her* children, *her* future, *her* dreams. Her apology gave me a big clue about the reason she had never found the motivation to get results. She didn't see it as HER business, or her future—she saw it as mine.

When you see your network marketing business as YOUR business, not only will your attitude completely change ... so will your results.

2. **Expectation**

A business is an investment, and any investor knows that it takes time for the harvest to yield after you sow. A business owner does not hold out their hand at the end of the first day of toil; but they know faithfully that they will reap in abundance, in time.

An employee, on the other hand, is in the habit of exchanging time for money. The transaction is linear: if I work these hours, I will get this much. Tragically, this mentality can make newcomers impatient, and they often forget one important fact: an employee gets paid once for each hour they work; a business owner may not get paid immediately, but they can get paid **forever.**

I remember the exact day the penny dropped for me. I was a few months into my business, when I went to my upline coach and sulked about the fact that I was making such little money. He looked me in the eyes and said, "Why do you say you've made so little when your business hasn't stopped paying you yet?"

And indeed, it hadn't, and it hasn't still. For the work I did in that first year, I am still reaping the benefits weekly. Just like an investment, you don't put your money in and then go back to check the following week if it's been worth it. You know that it is with the passage of time, that the investment will yield its true result.

With network marketing, your investment is not only paid in dollars—it is also paid in time. You put in time and, as long as you don't withdraw your investment, you'll make great dividends on the other side.

Time + Money = True Freedom.

3. **Results**

Finally, as obvious as it sounds to say it, there is a world of difference between the results achieved by someone tackling their network marketing business like a job or a chore, and someone who is pursuing it with the passion of an entrepreneur.

The world is hungry for direction. Building a successful network marketing business is about being able to shine a light into the darkness and show people that there is hope and a way out of their personal nightmare—if they choose to follow you *'this way'*.

I often tell my new team members to see themselves as a signpost for people. Freedom this way. Residual income this way. Community this way. Better health this way. Regardless of what product you offer, our industry is about transformation. You and I need to become experts at showing people what is on the other side. And let me give you a hint: it's not more work!

If you see your business like a job, then that's all you'll ever be able to offer. The great leaders, the big visionaries, don't see a job—they see a business and a pathway to true financial independence.

The world of network marketing is divided into these two categories: the ones who 'hope' this might be a good opportunity, and the others who KNOW it is. They wake up each morning and work for *their dreams*, not for their company or their leaders.

It's no surprise really, that the person with a mindset of personal leadership has the kind of energy that people want to follow, who will be a magnet for a large organisation and who ultimately will reach the mountain top.

CHAPTER THREE

You DON'T have to prospect family and friends

That's right. Yes, you heard right. You don't 'have' to prospect your friends and family to be successful in network marketing ... *but WHY wouldn't you?*

Imagine you just opened a new restaurant, or a new hair salon, or your own health spa. You're super proud of it, you're proud of your product or service ... wouldn't the FIRST people you'd invite to your new business **be** your friends and family? Or if someone in your family opened their new business, wouldn't you want to be the first person through the door to support it? Would it even matter what it was? Nope.

If my sister opened a taco truck, my kids are going to be eating tacos all the time. I've been loyal to the same dentist for years because he's a family friend. We pay a little more for our meat because we love our butcher and trust him with his quality. Most of us already make decisions about commerce based around relationships—it just makes common sense, and I don't get why your network marketing business should be any different.

Similarly, if you find a good deal, or you stumble across an amazing tip to save or to make money, wouldn't your family and friends be the very *first* people you'd tell about it? I'm

Latin American—if I *didn't* invite my family first, I'd be in trouble!

So why is it that when we jump into network marketing we suddenly become secret agents? It doesn't make any sense. Unless ... maybe you're not really sure that you're really onto something great.

The FIRST thing I wish I knew about network marketing before I got started (in case you skimmed through the first chapter), was that IT WORKS! If you knew with certainty and conviction that you hold in your hands the keys to your financial freedom and your time freedom, would you really have any issues bringing some of your closest people with you?

No, of course not. That's the reason why BELIEF changes everything. Belief takes away the fear, it takes away the barriers and hesitations. Belief makes you forget that you are prospecting, and makes you remember that you are *offering*. It turns you into someone others want to follow.

So, it's not that you don't want to talk to family and friends; *it's that you're not yet convinced that what you have to offer, is worth having.*

Also, for anyone who is still hung up about talking to their family and friends, I'd like to remind them that we are in "network" marketing—and by definition, in this great chosen profession of ours, we are called to *network*.

To reject the idea that we must learn to connect with people is kind of like being a dentist who would like to avoid touching teeth. Or an athlete who'd prefer not to work out. Or a singer who hates music. Well, you get the picture.

Building a global organisation, will require you to reach out to a few more people than your mom and your friend from yoga. I hope that isn't news to you! Most of your business, indeed, will be made up of complete strangers ... some of whom will *become* friends and family.

Nevertheless, let's all acknowledge that connecting with people and inviting them into our opportunity isn't always easy. You *will* be faced with rejection, you *will* be misunderstood. Welcome to the world of business. Tell me a business, any business in the world, which has a 100% uptake by potential prospects or customers? There isn't one. So, stop feeling like the world is conspiring against you, you're not *that* special ... you're just another entrepreneur dealing with the issues entrepreneurs have to deal with.

So, if that's the case, don't take it personally. Acknowledge that people WILL say no—sometimes more creatively than others—but welcome it as just a part of the process. Let go of any attachments to the outcome, release any effort from your part to *get* anyone to do anything. You're a signpost remember: *follow me this way*. If people want to go there great, if not, then you're looking for someone else.

Let go of the obsession to convince people. Instead, be convinced about what you've got. Give yourself a break and remember that there are over seven billion people in the world, and the decision of any one of them really doesn't alter the course of where you're going or impact your success. I don't care what product or service you are offering, I guarantee there IS a market for you. There are people sitting down at their computers *right now* typing questions into search engines, looking for the exact thing you have to offer!

How do I make money from home?

How do I get rid of this pain?

How to look younger / feel stronger?

How to work less hours?

How do I save more money?

How do I start my own business?

How do I reduce my debts?

They are out there. Our job is to find them. Do you remember a few years ago when 'fidget spinners' came out? If you don't know what one is, you probably don't have kids—because *every* kid had one. A fidget spinner is a silly little star shaped disc that you spin on your finger. They came in all colours and types of glitter, and for whatever reason, my kids felt it was essential to their very survival to own ALL of them. Every single one ever made.

Well, this is my point: if there's a market for something as pointless as a fidget spinner, there's probably a market for your product too. Can you just imagine the conversation that was had across the table when someone, sweating over their sketches inside some stuffy office, pitched the idea to the guy running the manufacturing plant?

"What is it?"

"It's a spinning thing."

"But what does it do?"

"It spins."

"But why would anyone want it?"

"To spin it."

I don't think the toy was a sensation due to any type of brilliance. The magic that got those little gadgets out of the factory and into millions of homes, is simply excitement and word of mouth. Kids told kids, who told kids. They went on TikTok, they passed them around with their friends, they learnt cool tricks and showed anyone who cared.

Yes, they told their *family and friends.* And when enough people tell their family and friends, that is how a product explodes across the world.

We can learn a lot from this. Seriously, kids are marketing machines. Forget all the strategies you can pick up over a four-year marketing degree, nothing (and I mean nothing) will ever out-perform the power of word of mouth— especially when it is fuelled by passion.

So, instead of stepping into your network marketing career like you're looking for 'prospects', go out into the world with the mindset that you are looking for people who share your **passions**. If you're excited about what you're offering, then go and find other people who are excited too.

Notice I said, they ARE excited too. Maybe they don't know about your company yet, but what you have to offer is something that matters to them already. You have a health product? Then stop throwing yourself at people who don't value their health. You can show someone how to make an income? Then stop throwing yourself at people who are happy staying broke.

When I first got started in network marketing, I wish I'd known that it wasn't my job to get people excited about anything. It was my job to connect with the people who were *already seeking* what I had to offer. I had to look for the people, who were already looking for me!

Whoa. That's a relief!

Finally, remember that as you sift and sort through the people who may, or may not, join you on your quest, every now and again you are going to discover a gem. Most people you talk to are forgettable, but some of the people you talk to will end up becoming your best friends. I love that!

I have friends in my network that once were nothing but the phone number of a cold contact on a list. Many years later, we are sitting at the pool bar in Mexico laughing about the way our lives have changed. Cherish people. They aren't just prospects—each one is a gift. Some will impact your life for a short time, others will stay with you for a lifetime.

As I travel the world these days and often find myself in some incredible places with many leaders from our team, I muse at how wonderful it is to be able to 'share success'. To reach a mountain summit with friends is far more rewarding than sitting at the top alone. Success shared, is success magnified.

So, BRING people on your adventure with you—firstly the people you care most about, then everyone else who wants to follow. They are out there, enjoy the process of discovering them.

CHAPTER FOUR

Objections are not a dead end, but a doorway

The imagination is an incredible thing. Do you remember being scared of something as a kid, only to realise later on that it was only your imagination?

I remember one morning when I was about seven, my little brother came running into the room in a panic, screaming hysterically that there was a bat in the house. I'd never seen a bat and I instantly imagined the worst: we were being hunted by a blood-thirsty flying demon!

We hid under the bed for what must have been an hour, until I finally decided we should venture out to inspect if the beast was still out there. Armed with pillows and shoes we crept out. To my total surprise, the 'beast' was nothing more than a tiny little cutie flapping around, desperate for a way to get out. In my mind, he had been Dracula.

We opened a window, and he was gone. And with him, our fear.

Often, the things in life that scare us, are not the *'thing'* itself, but our *'perception of the thing'*.

This is exactly what happens to us when it comes to objections. Think about it—when we feel afraid to prospect a person, the issue is not that we are afraid to 'make the contact'. What we're really worried about is having to face objections. And beyond that—the potential for rejection.

And yet if you think about it, our fear is absolutely irrational; because if we *don't* talk to someone, the answer is an automatic 'no' anyway. Instead of being rejected, we reject ourselves. We ensure that the worst possible outcome is a certainty.

However, just like with the little bat in the house, our fears can be reduced when we challenge our perception. Is an objection really such a bad thing?

What is an objection anyway?

An objection is not a barrier, it is simply information telling you what questions you need to answer next.

An objection is not a stop sign, it is an arrow pointing you towards your prospect's needs.

An objection is not a dead end, it is a doorway towards the next step.

If you can accept the information objectively, without ego or defensiveness, an objection can be your greatest ally. You don't *want* everyone. In fact, it's best if you don't *have* everyone. The time you waste working with the wrong people, is the time you didn't spend working with the right people.

As I wrote in the last chapter, remember *you're not on trial*. The business, the product, your team—*none of them are on trial*. The only one we are testing is the prospect. Are they a fit for what we are looking for, or not?

So, embrace objections for what they are. A sifting tool. Helping your prospects resolve their objections will allow you to separate the real players, from the tire kickers.

To help you along the way, be aware that there are three types of objections. Knowing the difference can save you a lot of time:

1. **Real objections:** these are rare, but every now and again your prospect is facing a real challenge (e.g., time or money shortage) and what they're really saying is, "please help me overcome this challenge". A great question to ask this prospect is, "If we could overcome that XYZ situation, would you have any reason not to jump in?"

2. **Impostor objections:** these are the most common. A prospect tells you one thing, but what they're really saying is something else. For example, "I don't have enough time," really means, "This isn't important enough to me … yet". Your job: get to the truth and help resolve their real concern, not their fake one.

3. **Projected objections:** are also very common. These are the ones you are subconsciously feeding your prospects. When I had no money, the majority of objections I received were about money. Why? Because I was projecting an energy of fear about the cost versus the value. My belief was weak, so I projected uncertainty. After I resolved that fear in myself, it stopped being a concern for others.

Whatever type of objection you are facing, I've found that the most effective way to break it down is to stop talking about the objection and start talking about the prospect instead. Their dreams, their goals, their hopes for the future. Aim to diagnose their greatest problems and offer them a tangible solution. Stop talking about you and *your* business—talk about *them*. After all, who is going to argue with you about themselves?

Stop trying to justify why network marketing is not a pyramid (ugh, I can't believe there are still people from the stone age who can't see that *their* workplace is more of a pyramid than any network marketing company will ever be). Sorry, I digress. Stop trying to justify why network marketing is not a pyramid and start talking about what your prospect needs instead.

"Sure, I understand. I had my hesitations too about the network marketing industry … let's put that aside and tell me Mary, what are you looking for in a business?" Then watch her describe exactly what we have to offer! She wants to work from home, spend time with her kids, have cashflow but flexibility, low entry level, support. Remember you're not there to convince anyone that they need what you have. Just help them figure out what they need and then see if you have a match.

This is exactly how I approach each contact today—and I wish I'd known this from the start. I go in with a mission to discover what they need most in their lives and then see if I can be the person that helps them accomplish it. Of all the many hats you'll wear as a network marking professional, this is the greatest. You and I are "transformation specialists". We help people go from where they are, to where they want to go.

Our mission in this industry is to offer them a pathway between both of those points.

At the end of the day, people are fascinating. We are all fragile, contradictory, dealing with our own fears and praying for our own dreams. Don't get upset if someone objects to you offering a solution to their problem, we are all incredibly good at getting in our own way.

Finally, the best way to overcome an objection is to talk to enough people so that you don't *have* to overcome every objection! Volume gives you choices, and having choices gives you posture.

Talk to one person each week and you put all the power in their hands. Talk to ten or twenty, and you're back in control of your destiny.

CHAPTER FIVE

Have a system or be the system

Let me ask you a question—would you prefer to be completely original, or would you rather be successful? Sometimes they are not mutually exclusive. In network marketing they are.

One of the advantages of network marketing, when compared to other business models, is the fact that there is already a *roadmap* to success. There's no need to re-invent the wheel or come up with a point of difference or figure things out yourself. The guesswork has been taken out of it, nobody is holding back the 'secrets to success'. You'll never be short of coaching and resources. *Why?* Because your leaders can't be successful if they don't show you how to do it too.

Still, it baffles me that many people getting started feel that they have to figure things out themselves. It's a little bit like having a Ferrari parked in the driveway but, instead of taking the keys and going for a drive, you decide to go build your own billy kart instead.

Sounds crazy, but so many of us come into network marketing like we are the first man or woman on the moon. We start trying things and experimenting, hoping that something will work—when it would be so much easier to follow a system that is already in place.

Let's step outside of network marketing for a moment and look at 'traditional' business. Instead of having people cheering for you to succeed, in traditional business you're more likely to have people hoping that you'll fail. In today's competitive marketplace, it's rare that anyone will give you access to trade secrets or coaching—and if they do, it will cost you.

In traditional business, there are generally only three ways to access proven systems for success:

Pay for a **franchise**. For a small six or seven figure fee you can purchase an established brand and benefit from a pre-established system. You get the security of a brand and track record, but at a very high price, inaccessible to most.

Pay for an **established business**. Purchase a business from someone who has already made all the mistakes and whose business is already up and running. Of course, there are no guarantees it will *keep* running once the person who built it moves on. By the way, you'll need to hand over between six to seven figures for this one also.

Pay for an **expert or business coach**. You'll pay anywhere from $300-$2000 an hour for a decent coach … and in most cases, they are coaching you from principles, but not necessarily from direct experience in your exact field. Coaching can be amazing, but it's important to know that the man with the experience is never at the mercy of the man with the theory. In other words, theory is great. Experience is better.

In each of the above examples, guidance and support in your new business venture comes at a cost. In network marketing, it's free, though sadly, not many people truly use it.

I wish I'd known this before I got started. I had been alone and in the wilderness for so many years, trying to fight my way forward as a single mom, that I almost didn't know how to accept help. More often than not, I'd had people tearing me down and it didn't seem to matter to anyone whether I made it or failed.

I've heard it said that one should never accept business advice from someone who doesn't have a direct vested interest in your success. In other words, don't take your investment tips from your work buddy who isn't sure how he'll pay next week's rent. Instead, pay close attention to the millionaires in your upline who have gotten to where they are, by helping thousands of others like you get the results you came for ... and who have a vested interest in your success.

The network marketing model is a perfect platform for teamwork. A person cannot succeed as an island. We succeed as a team. We succeed when we work to a system—no different to following the footsteps of someone who already knows the way up the mountain.

My first husband was someone who enjoyed adventure travel. One of the trips he decided to go on was to climb the highest mountain in Africa, Mt Kilimanjaro. Despite all the training that he and his team had, and all the fancy equipment, the most important part of their trip was to ensure they had selected good guides. A guide is a local who knows the mountain and who understands it's secrets and paths. Without a guide, even the world's best climbers could end up down the bottom of a crevasse.

As it turned out, they encountered great difficulty on that first climb and several of the team had to be brought back down from the mountain, due to severe cerebral edema. They recovered and were able to come back to make a second attempt at the summit—this time successfully. Had they not had the experience of local guides by their side, their adventure may have been fatal.

Many enthusiasts who decide to get started in network marketing and go it alone, end up with a similar fate: off the mountain and dead. Or at least their business is dead. You watch them start strong, but they fizzle out quickly as they flap about trying to survive, while their entire upline throws them lifelines. It's hard to watch ... and yet I've done it too.

We all think we're special, we all think we are unique. When I got started, I was convinced that the strategies being passed down to me might work for other people, but certainly not for me. My friends and family were surely different to everyone else, I was going to try a different approach ...

You know what happened? Nothing. Nothing at all, except I wore myself out and eventually was forced to reconsider. Maybe these multimillionaires trying to help me knew a thing or two. After all, what did I know? My way of doing things had left me broke and struggling ... maybe it was time to start trusting and following.

To be clear, this doesn't mean that we need to be robots. Nobody is suggesting that we let go of our personalities and our flair. We MUST be ourselves, but we should lean on the step-by-step system that has been shown to be a successful pathway to the top.

Working to an established system isn't just good news for you, but it's also good news for everyone getting started behind you. Instead of 'carrying' your team—you'll be able to show them a roadmap to follow.

What exactly is a system?

A system is a number of steps that have been proven time and time again to be the successful recipe to success. A system has generally been crafted out of lots of trial and error, thousands and thousands of hours of cumulative experience and observation.

Why mess with the recipe?

Unless you are the very first person to get started in your company, there is already someone in your upline who has gone before you and who has been successful. There are also, quite likely, a long line of people before you who were not successful.

We can learn from both. And from observing these patterns and principles your upline team has constructed a system to follow: how to set goals, how to make a plan, how to make a list, how to contact and get people started.

Sure, every team might do things a little differently. Just like there are many paths up the mountain … but the important point is that you're on a path that *works*.

There may be many pathways to success in network marketing. And there are many pathways that we also know will lead to failure: inconsistency, laziness, negativity. Following a system isn't just about being *on the right* path, it keeps you *off the wrong* path, too.

We all have habits that could hold us back if we don't replace them with new ones. We all have thinking that could block us if we don't learn new perspectives. I wish someone had pointed this out when I first got started. Accomplishing my goals was not going to be achieved merely through learning new things, but just as importantly, through *un*-learning the wrong things too.

My thinking was *broke thinking*. My self-belief and self-talk were holding me back. My habits were constantly sabotaging my progress. If I had any hope of improving my life, I had to start adopting new patterns of thinking and behaving. In short, I had to start observing and replicating the thinking and behaviour of those who already had the life I wanted.

I had to break up with my Bad Beliefs.

I remember one time in my twenties, visiting the home of one of the richest families in the country. As I wandered around their incredible mansion, I wondered, what had these people done that was so different to the choices most people make?

Not one to stay quiet, I found the moment to ask the husband the question, *"What do you believe that you have done* differently *to most people?"* He looked at me kindly and simply said, *"I think".* I was waiting for the rest of the story, but it never came. That was all of it—he spends time thinking every day.

Where most people spend time 'doing', he spends time reflecting, analyzing, and strategizing. I sipped on my champagne and nodded, wondering what *exactly* he thinks about.

Wouldn't it be amazing, I mused, to be able to have insight into the thoughts in his head that have taken him to great success? What are his strategies, what are his belief systems, how does he process things? What are his *secrets*?

Guess what? In network marketing, you don't have to wonder. Everyone's top secrets are on full display. Every Zoom meeting, every live event, every Facebook group, and every YouTube video is a powerful summary of knowledge that has likely taken years to accumulate.

It represents pain and effort that you can save yourself, because somebody else went through it for you.

You still have to make your own way on this journey, but if you choose a path that's well-worn, you're less likely to get lost.

CHAPTER SIX

Don't stress about leading thousands— learn to lead yourself

One of the questions I asked myself when I first got started in network marketing was, *'Will anybody follow me?"*

I mean, *why* would anybody follow me? Was I somebody worth following? I certainly didn't feel like I was. I was broke, tired, uncertain and my track record was a little tragic. Asking people to follow me felt like a big ask. I felt like an impostor.

But being someone people want to follow isn't about where you are today, it's about having clarity about where you're going tomorrow.

People follow momentum. Over the centuries people have rallied around visionaries who knew where they were going. Wars have been won this way. Companies have been formed this way. The entire world has been shaped this way.

And this is also how you can shape your world.

Contrary to what I first thought when I entered this industry, I don't have to become an expert at leading thousands, **I need to become an expert at leading myself.** That is the real key.

People who lack direction will lack followers. How can we motivate if *we* aren't motivated? How can we inspire if *we* aren't inspired? How can we lead if *we* aren't driven?

Did I mention that my sponsor was my ex-husband? I basically got started, just to get him off my back. Every time he would drop off the kids, he would mention this new business and I knew him well enough to know that my best option was just to sign up. Even though, deep down, I knew I had no intention of ever really building it.

I mean, who wants to follow their ex-husband into anything? We get along really well, but the last thing I thought I'd end up doing in my life was joining him in another business.

But here's what happened next. Even with my TOTAL reluctance to engage with the business, I couldn't help but *watch*. When you make a declaration that you're going somewhere, people will quietly watch you from the sidelines. Some are curious, some want to watch you fail to validate their own decision to do nothing ... and some will watch you 'just in case'.

Just in case you actually make it ... in which case they may have to re-evaluate their own decision.

You see, there are two important dates in your network marketing career: the day you sign up, and the day you actually get started. They're usually different days. Many people get started in network marketing—they show up to the party—so to speak, but then they leave because nothing much is happening. They were promised music and lights, but the crowd is dead. And so, they leave and sneak back to their quiet lives of artificial comfort in front of the television while they wait for their memberships to expire.

In my case, however, what I saw when I showed up to the party made me want to stay. My sponsor wasn't just full of hype, he was filled with passion. I watched as he and a handful of his leaders started to build momentum, grew a crowd, and started getting exciting results. I watched their lifestyles start to change, their conviction and organisations grow. Their homes, cars and vacations improved. I remember having this exact thought, *"Holy cow, I'm about to get left behind!"*

If I don't get moving *right now*, I'm going to be the cautionary tale: the woman who was given an extraordinary opportunity, but instead decided to work three jobs for the next 40 years of her life. No thanks!

Eighteen months later, I was earning six figures. Pretty awesome, but here's the real point I'm trying to make: nobody had to convince me, drag me, coerce me. The only thing that works in leadership is **example.** Show people where you are heading, and they will be inspired to follow! Become **proof** of who they can become and what they can accomplish.

It truly does come down to this: **we must become the people we are trying to find.**

When most of us start our careers in network marketing, we are often obsessed with the idea of finding a "great leader". I certainly was. As I sifted through prospects and potentials, I was like a miner looking for gold—certain that there was someone *'out there'* that could make me successful. Here is the thing I wish I'd known:

That 'someone' isn't *out there*. That 'someone' is *within*.

You and I already carry the seeds of greatness inside of us. Ugh, it sounds corny, but it's SO true. We all have incredible *potential*. There is a greater version of ourselves waiting to be released onto the world. It isn't something we need to find in others, it is something we need to unleash in ourselves. Just like the acorn is pre-destined to become a great oak, you have the potential to become a far greater version of yourself ... if you just don't get in the way.

Looking to lead others before you're able to lead yourself, will leave you frustrated. It's like trying to teach your kid to ride a bike, without knowing how to ride one yourself.

Obsessing over turning your new associates into great leaders is likely to leave you exhausted. Why? Because what we're doing is giving our power away. We've decided that we can only be successful based on the actions of others ... *when the only person we can control is the one staring back in the mirror.*

It's liberating, isn't it? Having to work on just one person (ourselves), instead of having to work on hundreds (your team). In the end, once you look back over your large global organisation, you'll realise that you didn't need to find replicas of yourself anyway. When I look at all my leaders, we couldn't be more different. We have different styles, different personalities, different strategies. What we share is a common passion and a common vision. We all saw the potential of this vehicle and believed it was the perfect pathway to our dreams.

How I wasted time at the beginning trying to make the wrong people into the right ones! When all I needed was to go out and find people who would recognise that where I was headed, was somewhere they wanted to go too. If I could go back and talk to myself in those early stages, I would tell myself to relax and stop trying to *find* leaders, and to throw my focus into *becoming* one instead.

Yeah, but ... I *need* to find leaders in my business, don't I?

Yes, you do. But you're the first one you need to find. You're the most important one. And let me tell you why: that little law that is working away quietly in the background of everything we do.

It's called **The Law of Attraction.**

The Law of Attraction, as explained by the great and late Bob Proctor in his masterpiece, *You Were Born Rich*, is **always** working. Just like gravity, you don't choose whether you turn it off or on. All you and I can choose is whether we work with it or we have it work against us.

Have you ever noticed that the person who walks around anticipating the worst luck, always gets it? Have you noticed that optimists seem to have charmed lives?

If you walk around telling yourself that life is tough ... life will keep getting tougher. If you walk around expecting that everything works out in your favour, it will. Why?

Because THOUGHTS ARE THINGS.

Though invisible to you and me, thoughts are tangible vibrations which interact with the world around you. Send enough of a particular thought out into the world, and the world will connect you with it. You've seen thousands of examples of this in your life ... and indeed if you really sit down and analyze it, your entire life is an example that this Law is in play.

Now that we know this, we need to **think very carefully about what we think!**

What this means in a practical sense, is that if you're spending a lot of your time worrying that nobody in your team is a leader, then the message you are projecting into your business is: *nobody in your team is a leader.*

Take a look at the status of your business and ask yourself this question, "What am I saying to myself about my business, that is *giving me* my business?"

- I can't find any leaders

- My customers never stay

- This business is hard to build

Whatever you're saying, it's a template for what is true.

Thousands of people have joined network marketing over the last ten years. They each have similar awesome products, similar positioning, similar markets, similar obstacles ... and yet, every person getting started in network marketing has a different experience.

We are the only variable. And yet, we usually waste so much energy trying to manage and control everything else ... but ourselves.

Some years ago, when my second son was around twelve, I found myself looking for a way to teach him this principle.

He was in a foul mood, complaining about everything. He was convinced that nothing was fair for him in our family and that he had it tougher than everyone else.

I went into his room and sat on the bed beside him and asked him to humour me with an exercise: take a look around the room and tell me everything you see that is yellow. He took a long sigh, and reluctantly named around eight or so items that were yellow.

I then asked him to close his eyes and keeping them closed, I asked him to name all the items in his room that were *blue*.

Blue? He hadn't been looking for blue. He took a guess; maybe there was a blue book somewhere? Perhaps there might be a shirt? In truth, he could hardly name anything blue. Then he opened his eyes and smirked—there was blue everywhere! Shoes, school bag, a poster ... even the bed cover we were sitting on was blue!

The lesson? **Our experience of life is driven by the perspective we seek to validate.** Whatever we are focused on, is what we will find. If we are focused on the obstacles, they keep turning up. If you focus on what you're not finding, you'll keep on 'not finding'.

Don't focus on finding. Focus on *becoming*.

It is the only thing that is really under our control. Taking back your power is liberating. Your success is not in the hands of anyone else, but your own.

Don't wait for a hero. Become one!

CHAPTER SEVEN

A goal is only a wish, until you make a plan

Every January, once the glitter from all the New Year's Eve parties has settled, people stumble into the bleary light of January with fresh enthusiasm, a notepad and pen ... ready to set new goals. *This* year is going to be different. I'm going to make a million bucks, I'm going to lose thirty pounds, I'll learn to play the trumpet and while I'm at it, I'll climb Mount Everest too. Yeah, add that to the list.

The list is written in a flurry, it gets crumpled into a drawer and is generally never seen again, until *next* January when you're looking for a notepad and pen to write your goals again. Funny how the new list looks surprisingly similar to the one we wrote last year because most of our goals remain unfulfilled ... fantasies on the horizon that we must inevitably dangle in front of ourselves once more.

Why does this happen? Why do some people accomplish their goals, and why do others just stare at them year after year?

Writing goals is great. In fact, it is *essential*. But it's only the first part. It's like jumping into a car and deciding where to go. You definitely need to know your destination ... but next you need to have a map. A goal without a map is little more than a wish. You can drive around for an entire year trying to get there, but without a clear roadmap you're likely to drive around in circles.

But I thought I just had to decide what I wanted, and let the Law of Attraction, or the 'universe' do the rest?

No. Not really. The Law of Attraction decrees that you and I will attract into our lives that the which we **believe** in. The problem is—it's hard to truly *believe* in something that your intellectual brain can easily dismiss. The point of mapping out your goals is not just a practical exercise, but a psychological one as well.

When you can see a possible pathway between where you are, to where you want to be, your confidence is activated. Your faith is lifted. Your excitement rises. Your belief grows stronger.

And when your belief is stronger, you are more likely to take action. Taking action leads you to start seeing results. Just the very act of being in motion, builds emotion. Confidence, passion, focus.

And so, a positive feedback cycle is born:

- Belief leads to Action
- Actions lead to Results
- More Belief leads to more Action ... and so on.

A goal without a plan is hard to invest in. You can put pictures of it all over your wall but, if you haven't broken your goal down into pieces, if there is no *roadmap*, your brain will hold it out in the distance as a fantasy and not a destination.

It's as futile as wanting to catch a fish, but you haven't yet put your rod in the water. It's very hard to believe in that big fish, when you haven't taken the first basic step.

So, what exactly is a plan?

A plan is a series of landmarks. It is a map of stepping stones between where you are today and where you need to be. It breaks down your goal into achievable and mentally believable portions. What do you need to accomplish, and by when, in order to be on track? What targets do I need to hit this year, this quarter, this month, this week … *today*— in order to be on track?

It's fantastic that you want to be a millionaire, but do you have a date for making your first $10,000? Do you know how many people you need to sponsor? How many meetings do you need to do this week? How many calls or messages sent daily?

The plan can be fluid. The plan might change along the way. You might miss goals, in fact I promise that you will … and that's okay. The plan is designed to be a compass not a contract. It allows you get back on track easily and allows you to stay engaged with your goal.

If we don't have a plan, it's hard to know when we are on track—and more importantly, when we are not. When I first got started building my business, one of my first dreams was to be able to generate $2000 per month. I knew that if I could do it, my rent would be covered. No matter what happened in my life, I would always have a roof over my head. It was a good goal.

Next came the roadmap. I went to my upline and asked them at what level I would be comfortably earning that amount and what would I have to do to get there. I was willing to do the work, I just really needed some clear instructions.

So we sat down and looked at some numbers; it was exciting! Looking at my plan on paper allowed me to feel empowered. It turned out that I didn't need five million people in my business. I needed to go out and sponsor 24, and then help some of those reach their own goals. Suddenly the $2000 per month that I needed to cover my house payments seemed attainable. I worked out that if I was sponsoring two people per week, I would be on track to reach my goal in three months.

Two people per week. Awesome, I can do that. I looked at my track record and calculated that in order to sponsor two people per week, I would have to at least talk to five people daily. Wait a minute ... I can do more than that. I'll talk to ten people per day. That way I can get there in half the time!

Breaking things down into daily activity targets had given me a massive boost in belief and confidence. It also gave me a sense of urgency and ownership. It wasn't up to 'luck' or fate. If I wanted to earn that income, all I had to do was go and get it.

Having a detailed plan also allows us to recover quickly when we go off track. If I missed a day, I could make up my numbers the next day. If I missed a week, it became critical to make sure the following week was better. Without a plan, however, it might have taken me months to realise when I was off track—and very likely that I would miss my goal altogether.

This is why good coaching is essential. A mentor who already knows the way will help you map out a strategy and help you stay accountable to your plan. This, I have found, is the key mistake we all make when it comes to planning. We confuse dreams for goals. We assume that because we know the destination, that the roadmap will automatically be clear. That's not the case.

I see good people, with great dreams, waste time every day. They're poking at their business timidly, hoping something magical will happen that will cause their business to explode. This will never work. Let's just get real. A strong dream demands a clear action-plan. If it's important to you, you *need* to have a plan, so you know what you need to do daily.

At the end of my workday, I ask myself only one question: "Did I move closer to my goal today, yes, or no?" I don't stress over people joining, people quitting, someone whining ... all I need to know to sleep well is, did I do MY part? Did I do what I needed to do? *Did I stick to the plan?* All the little things that happen daily are not important when you are working to a pre-determined plan.

So, what's your plan?

Knowing that you want to lose fifty pounds, doesn't mean you know what you need to eat and how many times you need to hit the gym. Set the target and then get help from a coach to set the plan. You want to retire from your job by Christmas? Great. Go to your upline and ask them to tell you exactly what it's going to take. Go about it like you're planning a heist. What are you doing, when are you doing it, what do you need to do it? Who are your allies? What tools will you need? What skills do you have to learn? Determine what the obstacles are and prepare for them.

Act like you mean it. Plan for it like you're serious. This is power.

A goal without a plan is a goal that is always in the distance, always "out there" in the future. The moment you have a plan, your goal is something you can start moving towards today.

CHAPTER EIGHT

Persistence always beats perfection

There were so many emotions I remember having when I first got started in network marketing. There was excitement, there was hope, there was quite a bit of fear … but most of all, there was confusion.

I didn't really understand the product, the compensation plan seemed like a giant puzzle, and I wasn't sure how to get started. I had the sneaking suspicion that it might take me an entire decade to learn everything I needed to know! It was paralyzing.

Lucky for me, I didn't have the luxury of staying paralyzed. I had absolutely no time to waste. I had four kids to feed, rent to pay and bills to deal with. I was afraid of getting things wrong, but I was MORE afraid of not getting *anything* done. I figured that moving forward while making mistakes, was better than not moving forward at all.

Don't let perfection get in the way of progress.

As it turns out, mistakes are not the by-product of growth, but it's *the way* to growth. If you're waiting for all the lights to go green before you embark on your journey, you'll never leave. Often in life, we are called to choose between perfection or progress. The only way to avoid making mistakes is to do nothing at all.

One of the key features of our industry is that you can get started without any preparation. It doesn't matter where you come from, or who you are. It doesn't matter how many degrees you have or don't have. Our apprenticeship happens on the job.

Everything you learn before you get started is useful, but not essential. Experience is the only true teacher. You can't refine your script, until you've messed it up a few times. You can't become a great presenter, without spending many hours sweating in front of a microphone.

One of the first meetings I did was via Zoom to a prospect in France. The lady in question was an osteopath and clearly more knowledgeable in health than I was. Everything in me told me not to do the meeting: my French was rudimentary at best; I would surely make a fool of myself. But a little voice also said, "But what if you miss a big opportunity?" So I reluctantly agreed.

The meeting went well. It wasn't perfect, but I survived. She was excited enough that she asked if I might do a meeting for a group of her colleagues. Oh, darn it. Just when I thought the nightmare was over, the stakes had risen. A *group* of medical professionals? Please no. Everything in me told me not to do the meeting: my French had barely held up, my product knowledge was basic, and I was absolutely guaranteed to make a fool of myself.

But there was that voice again. What if this was a big opportunity? What if saying 'no' turned out to be a huge mistake? Could I live with myself—passing up chances to get closer to a life I wanted so badly? So ... I said yes again and I'm glad I did because if I had said no, I would have never known that from this meeting would come my biggest group. Still today, that one meeting, which was completely imperfect, represents one of the most important meetings I've ever done.

But I also have done a lot of meetings that went nowhere. I've pushed myself at times where it hasn't paid off. Well that's life, that's business. But if you say "yes" enough times, you won't miss the ones that count.

Release yourself from the pressure of thinking that everything you do has to be perfect. Getting it right isn't what matters—what counts is showing up.

There isn't one single call or one single meeting that is *that* important. There isn't a single mistake you can make that will irreparably ruin your future. What counts is that you keep giving yourself options. Keep showing up: imperfect, clumsy, uncomfortable. Keep showing up. And every now and again, it will count. Really count.

Volume gives you choices. It also gives you perspective. The more you do, the less any one outcome matters. You are not successful because of what you do today, you are successful as a result of the things you do *every* day.

So wake up tomorrow and determine to be great at *not* being great. Get comfortable with missing shots. Learn to welcome the "no's" just as much as the "yes's" ... it's all progress. Everything you do wrong, moves you closer to being able to do it right.

Progress is what we are paid for—not perfection.

CHAPTER NINE

The rewards go to the dreamers

I hope it doesn't come as a shock to you if I let you know that success is going to take work. It will. To be completely honest, it will probably take a level of effort you've given very few things in your life—but only for a short time.

Don't let anyone tell you otherwise. The leaders you see sitting on the beach and travelling the word with their perfectly refreshed faces, probably walked around with dark circles for a while. They're smiling now, but I bet there were a few times all they could do was cry. They missed parties and vacations, they went low on sleep, they ate gas station food way too often, and probably slept on the cold floor of an airport in some town, the name of which they can't remember.

It's just the way it is. We don't talk about it enough, maybe we should.

It's called getting it done. It's called discipline.

And as I feel your body drain with the weight of this word— I'd like to give you some good news. You do not have to be disciplined to the work. Forget that. You just need to be disciplined to your *dream*.

Nobody ever woke up and jumped out of bed feeling totally motivated and inspired to make cold calls. The reason a leader jumps out of bed with excitement is because they are driven by the chance to get closer to their dream.

Inspiration does not require any preparation.

You don't need to be someone special, or have the right amount of training, or have the best quality contacts and all the right skills, in order to step into your business every day, inspired. Sure it's nice to have those things, but in truth, every advantage surrenders to the bigger question:

Do you have a dream?

If you do, you can get going right now. Right this very minute you can start inching a little closer towards it. You don't need to be any better, or any more knowledgeable or any more ready. You have all you need right now. Why?

Because the single most important attribute of a leader is Passion.

And Passion comes from Purpose.

Having a dream gives you the reason to learn the skills—if you don't have them. It gives you a reason to find the right contacts—if you don't know anyone. To develop into a leader—even if you're not ready.

Clarity of purpose absolutely trumps every single obstacle you face, because there is always a bigger reason to DO this—than there is *not* to do it.

If I could turn back time, I would change the questions I was constantly asking myself when I got started.

Questions like: Do I want to do this? Do I have the skills? Do I have the time? Am I the right kind of person to succeed?

These are all the WRONG questions. The only question that matters is:

Do I have a reason?

All other questions bow down and surrender to a dream.

Do I want to do this? *No, but I need to.*

Do I have the skills? *No, but I'll find them.*

Do I have the time? *No, but I'll make some.*

Am I the right kind of person? *Probably not, but I'll become her.*

Of all the keys to getting started, this is truly the most important one. Don't go into battle without a cause.

Find your reason and you'll find your path.

Anyone who knows me knows that, of all the things that I am, the most important one is being a wife and a mom. At the time I got started with my network marketing business, I was a single mom with nothing in the bank but big dreams in my heart.

One of the first things I did, when I decided to go 'Diamond' was to put up a big sign in the kitchen. I pinned a picture of my sons and wrote this message to myself above it: *You said you would do anything for these boys … so go Diamond.*

It was a daily reminder of why I was doing what I was doing. I knew that going Diamond would change our lives. It would allow us to live in a better house, drive a car that wasn't

falling apart, buy shoes that lasted, buy the groceries I wanted instead of the ones I could afford.

Every time I would feel tired, discouraged, or scared—I would force myself to look at the photograph of my boys and pull myself out of my pity party. Knowing my dream with clarity meant that I always had something to draw strength from. Sure I felt the weight of obstacles sometimes, but my love for those boys was always stronger. Looking at those four little faces would get me up off the floor each time, kept me moving forward and gave me an endless source of courage.

I remember I had pictures like that all through the house. One that I remember in particular was a picture I had cut out of a travel magazine of the Eiffel Tower in Paris. It had always been my dream to go; it seemed like an audacious goal, but it also symbolized freedom. I knew that if I could get to Paris with my boys, it would likely mean that my rent and the kids' shoes were covered. Paris represented *freedom*. Paris was the top of my Everest.

Visualizing myself looking up at the Tower with my arms around my babies would draw so much emotion from me, and I can tell you it did not disappoint. The day finally arrived where I was able to take my boys to Paris. The rent was no longer a problem, we had bought a house. Worrying about food and shoes was a faded memory. I stood on one of the most beautiful bridges of Paris at sunset, Pont Alexandre III, and looked across the River Seine to the beautiful Eiffel Tower in the distance; my beautiful boys beside me.

Tears running down my face, complete and absolute elation. Gratitude about how much our lives had changed. And their faces, oh my god, their little faces. Just filled with awe and inspiration. Mom made a promise to change our lives ... and she actually did. Maybe anything is possible. Dreams *do* come true, and this dream had driven me and sustained me through the tough times.

Don't ever dismiss the power of having a powerful vision.

So while we're pouring all our energy into trying to find the motivation to get up and do the work, we should instead be pouring our energy into connecting with our purpose. Not just finding a dream—but courting it. Put pictures on your wall, put images on your screen saver, visualize it, talk about it. Dream it.

Get to know it, spend time with it. Fall in love with it. Fight for it. It has to be something that chokes you up, something you can't help losing yourself in. It has to be something that will get you up off the floor, no matter how hard the punch.

I've always started and finished each day like this—playing out movies in my head, glimpses into my future. Walking through our new home, the smell of the new furniture, the lights over the pool. I've spent time dreaming about travelling the world with our children. Seeing their little faces light up as they walk through castles in Europe or ski at the best resorts.

I've imagined the feeling of true freedom. Lying in bed quietly, knowing that money is no longer a problem. I'm free of the worry, liberated from the stress. There's enough in the bank, there's enough every week—for whatever life we want. There's always enough.

To be honest, I've done this over and over in every area of my life. Before I met my amazing husband, I spent time imagining the perfect relationship in my mind. The safety, the happiness, the absolute completion of having met my best friend and my match.

Before having our own child, I spent long hours imagining what our little bundle would look like, the softness of his skin, the sweetness of his little feet. That magical moment when we would hold him for the first time.

The key is to *feel* it. Really commit to the visualization. Allow yourself to sink into it, experience it and connect with it. It is from this place of emotional connection that we start to send out a different message to the world—our vibrational energy shifts. We start attracting a new reality. Our thoughts become like lighthouses, guiding us home.

Dreaming may hurt at first. There will be a stubborn part inside of you that will resist it, clinging on to your current comfort zone for dear life. Until you start seeing small shifts in your reality, serendipities, and coincidences, as your new world starts to align.

Becoming the true architect of your own life is addictive. Realizing that you are truly in control of your own reality is one of life's most powerful revelations. You can live perfectly in the present but be equally delighted about what's to come. As you start to learn to drive this powerful Law of Attraction—you'll never want to stop.

It's the birthplace of your tomorrow. It's the highest calling of being human: to have creative power over our destiny.

The rewards go to those who dare to dream.

CHAPTER TEN

Grow—or get left behind

It is a truth, universally acknowledged, that in order to have more in our lives—we must first *become* more. When I first came to network marketing, I arrived with baggage. Invisible baggage of course, but very heavy baggage, nonetheless.

I had spent almost a decade in the 'wilderness', bouncing from job to job, getting up after one failed project to the next. I felt like I had spent years knocking on doors that never opened. My experiences had led me to accumulate a set of beliefs about me ... or rather:

My beliefs about myself had led me to accumulate a set of experiences.

We live the life that we accept. I looked in the mirror and I had stopped seeing 'possibility'. I accepted myself as a struggling single mom, someone who never had enough and who never got a break. So even if an opportunity did come my way, my first instinct was to sabotage it: "No, it's probably not real. It won't work for me. I don't have time. I don't have money. I don't have what it takes ... ".

It turns out that we're incredibly creative when it comes to coming up with excuses to protect our 'equilibrium'. What I mean is, it's easier to come up with a list of reasons why you can't change ... than to actually change. Change can be challenging, painful even. From an evolutionary perspective, change is *dangerous*.

Think about two cavemen—let's call them Johnny and Bill. Johnny asks Bill if he wants to go exploring over the hill. Bill says no, and quickly reminds him that their buddy, Larry, went over the hill and got eaten by a saber-toothed tiger last week. Exploring is dangerous. Johnny sighs and offers Bill some red berries instead. Again, Bill declines. Is Johnny crazy? Doesn't he remember that Jenny tried berries last week then died a gruesome death on the cave floor?

From the beginning of time, trying new things has been dangerous. So, we become programmed to avoid risk. Risk equals danger. It's safer for things to stay the same.

That's all well and good except that without change, nothing changes. Duh. If Johnny and Bill never tried new things, we'd still be living in caves. All progress involves risk. Evolution, by definition, is *change*.

Yet many of us still try to cheat the rules. We want to change our lives, without having to change ourselves. We want it all—but want to give nothing.

Our dreams call us to change, but we try to negotiate instead. Do I really want that new house, or is it just going to be more cleaning? Do I really want more income when it just means I have to pay more tax? (Yes, I've actually heard people say this!) Do I really need to travel the world and see the Eiffel Tower? When I can get croissants at my local bakery …

We tell ourselves these soft lies as a type of balm to soothe the wounds that are left behind by unfulfilled dreams. It's easier to convince ourselves that we want nothing, then we don't have to risk anything. It's easier to shrink back into our shells and forget about the exciting life that awaits us, if only we dared to chase it.

In network marketing, it's much more comfortable to tell yourself that, "this business probably won't work for me", than admit that, "this business has worked for other people, and it would most likely work for me, if I decided to stop blaming everyone else and took responsibility for my life". Ouch.

Ouch, but true.

Even if we're not aware of it, we all have a set of belief systems too—a narrative we have put in place about who we really are. It spins around like a broken record touching every decision we make, like it were the theme music to our lives. These sets of beliefs are either holding us back or propelling us forward. Look at the areas with momentum in your life; the clues are already there. If you're thriving at your job, it's probably because you 'believe' you're really good at it. If you're having an amazing marriage, it's probably because you believe your spouse is a legend and relationships are fun.

Pay close attention: most of us get this causal relationship back to front. It is a MAJOR misconception which costs us dearly. We assume that the thoughts we have are the result of what happens in our life BUT, actually, *what happens in our lives is the result of the thoughts we allow ourselves to have.*

The good news: you can change your thoughts any time.

And this ... is truly the secret to changing our lives.

Most of us find ourselves chipping away at circumstances, trying to "fix" things, without first cleaning up our thoughts. In case you haven't worked it out, it's a hopeless battle. It's the same as trying to put out a fire, while you're still pouring fuel!

Walk up to a mirror right now and ask yourself these super scary questions: Who Am I? What do I really believe about myself? What do I really believe I can accomplish? What kind of life am I willing to accept?

We get in life, not what we want ... we get in life what we **expect.** Read that again.

When you start to unpack the truth buried within your belief systems, you'll start to reveal the blind spots that have been holding you back. Once you've identified your belief systems, you can go after them—literally target them with your personal growth.

I once took my children for a walk in the forest to explain the importance of embracing growth. I carried a brick all the way to an empty field and laid it on the ground. I asked the boys to step back and watch. With a little bit of fanfare, I asked them this question, "How long will it take for this brick to become a wall?"

They looked at each other with confusion; our mother has finally lost her marbles. It was bound to happen sooner or later. I asked them a new question, "How long will it take for this brick to become a house?" Again, more strange looks.

With even more flair, I asked one last question, "What about a cathedral? How long should we wait for this brick to turn into a cathedral?" A quiet little voice finally piped in, "Never, Mom. It's never going to turn into anything all by itself."

Exactly! I jumped up with excitement and made my point: *Time alone changes nothing*. Just because time passes, it doesn't mean that you become smarter, stronger, or richer. Your life won't improve spontaneously over time without intervention. We won't grow into better people without making an effort—a *choice*.

Growth is a deliberate decision. A cathedral is built brick-by-brick, just like we are built by the sum of all our choices. Use books like weapons. Attend events, get around the right people, find a coach, write and review affirmations daily ... search out areas where your beliefs are weak, and make a deliberate choice to build better beliefs daily. I remember hearing Tony Robbins speak about making the decision to change his life. He knew he needed to radically change his mindset and so he powered through 700 books, hungry to change his thinking. Like a beautiful cathedral in construction, you and I are choosing to build, or to destroy, every day.

You and I are a work in progress. Every day is an opportunity for growth: physical, mental, emotional, spiritual. Love yourself today but be excited about who you can be tomorrow. Don't accept the current version of yourself as the final masterpiece. You are today but an inspired blueprint of the true greatness that you could become tomorrow.

Challenge your perceptions. Invite new perspectives. Don't accept your own thoughts as Law. Be open to new possibilities. Question how you respond, and how you react. Observe yourself and try on new thinking. New habits. Most of all ... new beliefs.

Why? Because if we are not growing, we are already dying.

Stop being afraid of change and become excited about growth. Take intentional steps towards becoming more and you'll see a brand new, far more exciting, life unfold.

I wish you well on your journey. I promise it will be worth the climb.

With love,
Cristina

Final thoughts

So, here you are. You have some stuff to think about. How are you feeling? Are you excited? Are you nervous? Hopeful? Overwhelmed? Excited?

Maybe all of the above.

However you're feeling, I just want to leave you with one thought: you are **ready.**

No matter who you are or what crazy past you've come from, I want you to know that you CAN do this. There is no obstacle in the way. The path is clear, and your dreams are truly within reach.

You don't have to uncover a secret code or become anyone super special … there is nothing you are "missing". You just need to be one thing: *hungry.*

You just need to want this badly enough. That's all.

If you have a strong enough emotional goal—you, my friend, are good to go. You're ready, just as you are. You don't need to be more prepared, or any more confident or anything other than **exactly** who you are.

I know I'm repeating myself, but, whatever. This is important. Maybe **the** most important fact to get through your sweet little head. And by the way, this isn't a pep talk—this is TRUTH.

You—yes, *you*—can start from wherever you are and create whatever life you've been dreaming of. You don't need to have more details about the compensation plan, you don't need to be a social media guru, you don't need to be a better public speaker, be prettier or have a more supportive partner. If you want this badly enough, everything (and I promise everything) will surrender to your Dream. You will always find a way.

I know you probably still have a lot of questions. But I promise you that you already have all the answers. If you've got a clear and powerful Dream, **that** is the answer to everything.

"I don't have time … I don't know what to say … I don't know where I'll find the people …".

If you know what is driving you, you will always have an answer and it will generally be a version of: *"who cares"* … *"I'll figure it out"* … *"someone will teach me"* … *"I'll do it anyway"*.

The point is, you don't need to know exactly HOW you'll do this. You just need to have laser focus as to WHY you need to get this done.

I've seen all kinds of types make it big over the years. From super-confident blond-bombshells to quiet little housewives. I've seen powerful professionals and also struggling single mums. I've seen highly educated professors and doctors, as well farmers that never finished school.

What I'm saying is, release yourself from the pressure of trying to be anything other than exactly who you are now.

Stop acting like you're deficient, missing something or waiting on someone. There is a place for you right here. Right *now*.

Again, all you need to be is *hungry*.

So, if you must spend time on anything, spend time on your dream. Stop worrying about what you don't have and start dreaming about what is coming. Stop wasting your time being scared about what you don't know and start focusing on the future that you *know* is certain.

Spend time with your future self. Get to know her/him. Yes, this is about to sound corny, but ... *fall in love* with who you *know* you can be.

That person is so awesome. That person isn't worried about things being hard or people saying no. That person probably isn't sure HOW they got it all done in the end. That person only knows WHY.

Know what you want. Believe in it. Go get it. *Period.*

That is really all there is to it.

About the Author

Meet Cristina Williams...

Cristina Williams is a businesswoman and mother, passionate about supporting dreamers and entrepreneurs in achieving their full unbridled potential and living big, wholehearted unapologetic lives.

Cristina emigrated to Australia as an El Salvadorian refugee in the late 80's and has overcome many personal difficulties, including a difficult divorce and raising four young boys with little resources. Cristina rebuilt her life, emotionally and economically, through the power of personal development and the vehicle of network marketing.

In the last few years, Cristina has travelled the world extensively, both professionally and personally, most recently living for a year in the South of France. She now resides with her husband and their seven sons in Arizona, USA.

Cristina is a business coach and public speaker, with a deep love of life who believes that we must all strive for personal excellence and fulfilment through the passionate pursuit of our dreams.

As a writer, Cristina has been active in the film industry, blogs, business articles and poetry—this is her first book.

It won't be her last.

Acknowledgements

This book is probably not finished and will never be finished. There will never be a day where I can say with finality, *"Here is the list of everything I wish I had known before I got started"*. The list is always changing but some things will always be the same.

First on that list, is my absolute gratitude and love for my husband, Mat. I have had books in my head my whole life, but only beside him have I felt brave enough to put them to paper. Thank you for being the person in my life who always sees a better version of me than I can. Thank you for always listening to my stories; you are by far, the greatest one.

Secondly, thank you to our beautiful tribe of sons. You, my boys, are the absolute reason why I woke up every day for years, ready to fight for our dreams. You gave me a vision and the fuel I needed to pursue a better life. You are the reason why, when I was falling, I realised I had no option but to learn to fly.

Thirdly, I am as always filled with gratitude to all my mentors along the way—too many to mention, but it's worth a try. Mal Sword, Dan Doyle, Bart & Melissa Kotter, Ed & Rebekah Wiens, Chuck & Tammi Gates, Deni & Tom Robinson, Bob and Trish Schwenkler, and all my other friends and cousins in the network marketing industry. You have each been instrumental pieces of the puzzle that I needed to solve to re-build my life. You inspire me daily.

Finally, I am thankful to the biggest dreamers I know: my beautiful parents. You leaped and took chances, even when you knew you might fall. We watched you fight back from all obstacles; you got up each time, stronger and wiser. You never, not for one second, ever gave up your dreams. Know that we, your children, were watching. We owe every single triumph in our lives entirely to you both.

And above all, I am thankful to the greatest mentor of all, my God above, who continues to bless us and teach us in more ways than we could ever count.

"He shall cover you with his feathers, and under His wings you will find refuge."

Psalm 91:4

He always has.

What's next from Cristina Williams?

Next book — *Breaking up with Bad Beliefs*

Affirmations, visualisation, and positive thinking ... they just don't work, do they? Well, at least not on their own.

Otherwise almost everyone who has ever set a goal would be wildly successful. We'd all be living in big houses, travelling the world, and laughing all the way to the bank. But most of us aren't.

Most of our dreams go unanswered and it is my deep conviction that it is not enough to try to adopt new beliefs, but that it is even *more* important to learn how to break up with old ones. It's like starting a new relationship; how could we ever hope to have a successful relationship with a new partner, whilst still sneaking around with the toxic ex?

I spent many years of my life dreaming about a different life, building dream boards and making lists of goals ... *that I knew deep down I would never have.* With my mind I was projecting my "intention" but with my heart I was projecting a very different emotional vibration (credit to the great Dr Joe Dispenza for this revelation).

The honest truth was that deep down in my heart, I was filled with doubts. I was insecure, afraid, wounded. I felt small, unworthy, unable. Affirmations and visualisations were never going to be enough.

Not until I realised that I first had to break up with Bad Beliefs. I had to let go of the self-sabotaging thinking that was holding me back.

In my years of coaching, I have found that I wasn't alone. This tragic pattern repeats over and over. Most people aren't held back from their dreams because they can't set goals for the future, they are held back because they have emotional and psychological attachment to their past.

That's why in my next book, *Breaking Up with Bad Beliefs,* I will show you exactly how to finally let go of the thinking that is holding you back. It is not a super complicated philosophical book (hopefully you can see by now that this is not my style), but it will be a practical manual to help you break the anchors that will allow you to finally, and peacefully, move forward.

I'm so excited about this next book. This process changed my life and set me free, and I hope that it will help you break into a better future too.

With love,
Cristina

Stay in Touch with Cristina

If you would like to stay connected with Cristina, please visit her website and join her mailing list. You'll be the first to hear about any new releases, articles or courses.

Alternatively, feel free to email Cristina directly. She would love to hear your feedback on the book and how it has made a difference on your journey!

WEB: www.cristinawilliamsauthor.com

Email: hello@cristinawilliamsauthor.com

Made in the USA
Monee, IL
24 February 2023

28614989R00056